Devlin

by Iain Gray

Lang**Syne**
PUBLISHING
WRITING *to* REMEMBER

LangSyne

PUBLISHING

WRITING *to* REMEMBER

Vineyard Business Centre,
Pathhead, Midlothian EH37 5XP
Tel: 01875 321 203 Fax: 01875 321 233
E-mail: info@lang-syne.co.uk
www.langsyneshop.co.uk

Design by Dorothy Meikle
Printed by Ricoh Print Scotland
© Lang Syne Publishers Ltd 2011

ISBN 978-1-85217-301-2

Devlin

MOTTO:
The cross is my star.

CREST:
A griffin and an Irish Cross.

NAME variations include:
Ó Doibhilin (*Gaelic*)
Ó Duibhlin (*Gaelic*)
O'Dobhalen
O'Develin
O'Devlin
Davlin
Defflin
Develin
Devline
Devolin
Devoline

Chapter one:

Origins of Irish surnames

**According to an old saying, there are two types of Irish –
those who actually are Irish and those who wish they were.**

This sentiment is only one example of the allure that the
high romance and drama of the proud nation's history holds
for thousands of people scattered across the world today.

It's a sad fact, however, that the vast majority of Irish
surnames are found far beyond Irish shores, rather than on
the Emerald Isle itself.

The population stood at around eight million souls in
1841, but today it stands at fewer than six million.

This is mainly a tragic consequence of the potato
famine, also known as the Great Hunger, which devastated
Ireland between 1845 and 1849.

The Irish peasantry had become almost wholly reliant
for basic sustenance on the potato, first introduced from the
Americas in the seventeenth century.

When the crop was hit by a blight, at least 800,000
people starved to death while an estimated two million
others were forced to seek a new life far from their native
shores – particularly in America, Canada, and Australia.

The effects of the potato blight continued until about
1851, by which time a firm pattern of emigration had
become established.

Ireland's loss, however, was to the gain of the countries in which the immigrants settled, contributing enormously, as their descendants do today, to the well being of the nations in which their forefathers settled.

But those who were forced through dire circumstance to establish a new life in foreign parts never forgot their roots, or the proud heritage and traditions of the land that gave them birth.

Nor do their descendants.

It is a heritage that is inextricably bound up in the colourful variety of Irish names themselves – and the origin and history of these names forms an integral part of the vibrant drama that is the nation's history, one of both glorious fortune and tragic misfortune.

This history is well documented, and one of the most important and fascinating of the earliest sources are *The Annals of the Four Masters*, compiled between 1632 and 1636 by four friars at the Franciscan Monastery in County Donegal.

Compiled from earlier sources, and purporting to go back to the Biblical Deluge, much of the material takes in the mythological origins and history of Ireland and the Irish.

This includes tales of successive waves of invaders and settlers such as the Fomorians, the Partholonians, the Nemedians, the Fir Bolgs, the Tuatha De Danann, and the Laigain.

Of particular interest are the *Milesian Genealogies*,

because the majority of Irish clans today claim a descent from either Heremon, Ir, or Heber – three of the sons of Milesius, a king of what is now modern day Spain.

These sons invaded Ireland in the second millennium B.C, apparently in fulfilment of a mysterious prophecy received by their father.

This Milesian lineage is said to have ruled Ireland for nearly 3,000 years, until the island came under the sway of England's King Henry II in 1171 following what is known as the Cambro-Norman invasion.

This is an important date not only in Irish history in general, but for the effect the invasion subsequently had for Irish surnames.

'Cambro' comes from the Welsh, and 'Cambro-Norman' describes those Welsh knights of Norman origin who invaded Ireland.

But they were invaders who stayed, inter-marrying with the native Irish population and founding their own proud dynasties that bore Cambro-Norman names such as Archer, Barbour, Brannagh, Fitzgerald, Fitzgibbon, Fleming, Joyce, Plunkett, and Walsh – to name only a few.

These 'Cambro-Norman' surnames that still flourish throughout the world today form one of the three main categories in which Irish names can be placed – those of Gaelic-Irish, Cambro-Norman, and Anglo-Irish.

Previous to the Cambro-Norman invasion of the twelfth century, and throughout the earlier invasions and settlement of those wild bands of sea rovers known as the Vikings in the eighth and ninth centuries, the population of the island was relatively small, and it was normal for a person to be identified through the use of only a forename.

But as population gradually increased and there were many more people with the same forename, surnames were adopted to distinguish one person, or one community, from another.

Individuals identified themselves with their own particular tribe, or 'tuath', and this tribe – that also became known as a clann, or clan – took its name from some distinguished ancestor who had founded the clan.

The Gaelic-Irish form of the name Kelly, for example, is Ó Ceallaigh, or O'Kelly, indicating descent from an original 'Ceallaigh', with the 'O' denoting 'grandson of.' The name was later anglicised to Kelly.

The prefix 'Mac' or 'Mc', meanwhile, as with the clans of the Scottish Highlands, denotes 'son of.'

Although the Irish clans had much in common with their Scottish counterparts, one important difference lies in what are known as 'septs', or branches, of the clan.

Septs of Scottish clans were groups who often bore an entirely different name from the clan name but were under the clan's protection.

In Ireland, septs were groups that shared the same name and who could be found scattered throughout the four provinces of Ulster, Leinster, Munster, and Connacht.

The 'golden age' of the Gaelic-Irish clans, infused as their veins were with the blood of Celts, pre-dates the Viking invasions of the eighth and ninth centuries and the Norman invasion of the twelfth century, and the sacred heart of the country was the Hill of Tara, near the River Boyne, in County Meath.

Known in Gaelic as 'Teamhar na Rí', or Hill of Kings, it was the royal seat of the 'Ard Rí Éireann', or High King of Ireland, to whom the petty kings, or chieftains, from the island's provinces were ultimately subordinate.

It was on the Hill of Tara, beside a stone pillar known as the Irish 'Lia Fáil', or Stone of Destiny, that the High Kings were inaugurated and, according to legend, this stone would emit a piercing screech that could be heard all over Ireland when touched by the hand of the rightful king.

The Hill of Tara is today one of the island's main tourist attractions.

Opposition to English rule over Ireland, established in the wake of the Cambro-Norman invasion, broke out frequently and the harsh solution adopted by the powerful forces of the Crown was to forcibly evict the native Irish from their lands.

These lands were then granted to Protestant colonists, or 'planters', from Britain.

Many of these colonists, ironically, came from Scotland and were the descendants of the original 'Scotti', or 'Scots', who gave their name to Scotland after migrating there in the fifth century A.D., from the north of Ireland.

Colonisation entailed harsh penal laws being imposed on the majority of the native Irish population, stripping them practically of all of their rights.

The Crown's main bastion in Ireland was Dublin and its environs, known as the Pale, and it was the dispossessed peasantry who lived outside this Pale, desperately striving to eke out a meagre living.

It was this that gave rise to the modern-day expression of someone or something being 'beyond the pale'.

Attempts were made to stamp out all aspects of the ancient Gaelic-Irish culture, to the extent that even to bear a Gaelic-Irish name was to invite discrimination.

This is why many Gaelic-Irish names were anglicised with, for example, and noted above, Ó Ceallaigh, or O'Kelly, being anglicised to Kelly.

Succeeding centuries have seen strong revivals of Gaelic-Irish consciousness, however, and this has led to many families reverting back to the original form of their name, while the language itself is frequently found on the fluent tongues of an estimated 90,000 to 145,000 of the island's population.

Ireland's turbulent history of religious and political strife is one that lasted well into the twentieth century, a landmark century that saw the partition of the island into the twenty-six counties of the independent Republic of

Ireland, or Eire, and the six counties of Northern Ireland, or Ulster.

Dublin, originally founded by Vikings, is now a vibrant and truly cosmopolitan city while the proud city of Belfast is one of the jewels in the crown of Ulster.

It was Saint Patrick who first brought the light of Christianity to Ireland in the fifth century A.D.

Interpretations of this Christian message have varied over the centuries, often leading to bitter sectarian conflict – but the many intricately sculpted Celtic Crosses found all over the island are symbolic of a unity that crosses the sectarian divide.

It is an image that fuses the 'old gods' of the Celts with Christianity.

All the signs from the early years of this new millennium indicate that sectarian strife may soon become a thing of the past – with the Irish and their many kinsfolk across the world, be they Protestant or Catholic, finding common purpose in the rich tapestry of their shared heritage.

Chapter two:

The cross and the star

A clan with an illustrious pedigree, septs of the Devlins were to be found from earliest times at different locations throughout Ireland.

The Gaelic form of the name is Ó Doibhilin or Ó Duibhlin, indicating a descent from one Doibhilin, or Duibhlin, but the true meaning of the name has unfortunately become obscured in the dim mists of Irish time.

Some sources assert it indicates someone with black hair, while others claim it stems from 'unlucky', or even 'boisterous.'

But bearers of the name today may prefer another theory that it denotes 'valour' or 'bravery'.

Devlins were to be found in present day Co. Sligo, where a Gillananaev O'Devlin is recorded as having held the honoured position of Standard Bearer to the O'Connor chiefs.

But it is further north, in the present day county of Tyrone in the ancient province of Ulster, that Devlins stamped an indelible mark on the island's history.

An area known as Munterdevlin, on the shores of the hauntingly beautiful Lough Neagh, was their territory.

It was here that they flourished for centuries as part of the powerful tribal grouping known as the northern Uí Neill

– a fact that highlights that they were of truly royal race, descended from Niall Noíghiallach, better known to posterity as the great warrior king Niall of the Nine Hostages.

The dramatic life and times of this ancestor of the Devlins are steeped in stirring Celtic myth and legend.

The youngest son of Eochaidh Mugmedon, king of the province of Connacht, his mother died in childbirth and he was brought up by his evil stepmother Mongfhinn who, for reasons best known to herself, was determined that he should die.

She accordingly abandoned him naked on the Hill of Tara, inauguration site of the Ard Rí, or High Kings, of Ireland, but a wandering bard found him and took him back to his father.

One legend is that Mongfhinn sent Niall and his four brothers – Brian, Fiachra, Ailill, and Fergus – to a renowned prophet who was also a blacksmith to determine which of them would succeed their father as Ard Rí.

The blacksmith, known as Sitchin, set the lads a task by deliberately setting fire to his forge.

Niall's brothers ran in and came out carrying the spearheads, fuel, hammers, and barrels of beer that they had rescued, but Niall staggered out clutching the heavy anvil so vital to the blacksmith's trade.

By this deed, Sitchin prophesied that Niall would be the one who would take on the glorious mantle of kingship.

Another prophetic incident occurred one day while Niall and his brothers were engaged in the hunt.

Thirsty from their efforts they encountered an ugly old woman who offered them water – but only in return for a kiss.

Three of the lads, no doubt repelled by her green teeth and scaly skin, refused. Fiachra pecked her lightly on the cheek and, by this act, she prophesied that he would one day reign at Tara – but only briefly.

The bold Niall, however, kissed her fully on the lips. The hag then demanded that he should now have full sexual intercourse with her and, undaunted, he did so.

Through this action she was suddenly transformed into a stunningly beautiful young woman known as Flaithius, or Royalty, who predicted that he would become the greatest High King of Ireland.

His stepmother later tried to poison him, but accidentally took the deadly potion herself and died.

This legend relates to what was known as the Festival of Mongfhinn, or Feis na Samhan (the Feast of Samhain), because it was on the evening of October 31, on Samhain's Eve, that the poisoning incident is said to have taken place.

It was believed for centuries in Ireland that, on Samhain Eve, Mongfhinn's warped and wicked spirit would roam the land in hungry search of children's souls.

The Festival, or Feast, of Samhain, is today better known as Halloween.

Niall became Ard Rí in 379 A.D. and embarked on the series of military campaigns and other daring adventures that would subsequently earn him the title of Niall of the Nine Hostages.

The nine countries and territories into which he raided and took hostages for ransom were the Irish provinces of Munster, Leinster, Connacht, and Ulster, Britain, and the territories of the Saxons, Morini, Picts, and Dalriads.

Niall's most famous hostage was a young lad known as Succat, son of Calpernius, a Romano-Briton who lived in the area of present day Milford Haven, on the Welsh coast.

Later known as Patricius, or Patrick, he became renowned as Ireland's patron saint, St. Patrick, responsible for bringing the light of Christianity to the island in the early years of the fifth century A.D.

Raiding in Gaul, in the area of Boulogne-sur-mer in present day France, Niall was ambushed and killed by one of his treacherous subjects in 405 A.D.

But his legacy survived through the royal dynasties and clans founded by his sons and that flourished as the tribal groupings of both the northern Uí Neill and the southern Uí Neill.

As part of the northern Uí Neill the Devlins owed fealty to the O'Neill chieftains, and this meant that they shared not only in their glorious fortunes but also their tragic misfortunes.

Misfortune certainly came to Ireland in the wake of the

late twelfth century Cambro-Norman invasion of the island, and the subsequent consolidation of the power of the English Crown.

English dominion over Ireland was ratified through the Treaty of Windsor of 1175, under the terms of which native Irish chieftains were only allowed to rule their territory as vassals of the English king.

But the province of Ulster proved particularly stubborn for a number of centuries in attempting to resist the power of the Crown.

It is recorded how in 1260, for example, the Devlin chieftain known as The O'Devlin was among the many native Irish killed by a force of English colonisers at the battle of Downpatrick.

Also among the dead was the O'Neill chieftain Brian O'Neill, whose head was cut off and sent in triumph to England's Henry III.

But not all Devlins were to be found on the battlefield.

An O'Devlin is recorded as having been an early thirteenth century Bishop of Kells, while the Devlins are also thought to have been responsible for the execution of the magnificent Ardboe High Cross, in Co. Tyrone.

Made of red sandstone and standing at about 18ft in height, the cross is considered to be one of the finest examples of the Irish High Cross.

Thought to have been sculpted and erected in the late ninth or early tenth century and standing proud on a small hillock near the west shore of Lough Neagh, it features 22 carved panels of Biblical events that include David slaying Goliath and the early life of Christ.

Officially listed as a National Monument of Northern Ireland, it is from this cross that the Devlin motto of 'The cross is my star' and crest of a griffin and an Irish Cross are considered to have derived.

Small chips have been removed from the ancient and weather-beaten Cross of Ardboe over the centuries – taken by locals to remind them of their heritage and homeland as they were impelled in the face of oppression and starvation to seek a new life on foreign shores.

No doubt descendants of Devlins living today in North America or other far-flung parts still retain these poignant reminders of the Emerald Isle.

Chapter three:
Penal policies

One indication of what became the increasingly harsh treatment meted out to native Irish clans such as the Devlins following the Treaty of Windsor can be found in a desperate plea sent to Pope John XII by Roderick O'Carroll of Ely, Donald O'Neill of Ulster, and a number of other Irish chieftains in 1318.

They stated: 'As it very constantly happens, whenever an Englishman, by perfidy or craft, kills an Irishman, however noble, or however innocent, be he clergy or layman, there is no penalty or correction enforced against the person who may be guilty of such wicked murder.

'But rather the more eminent the person killed and the higher rank which he holds among his own people, so much more is the murderer honoured and rewarded by the English, and not merely by the people at large, but also by the religious and bishops of the English race.'

This appeal to the pope failed to alleviate the plight of the native Irish, and matters only became much worse through a policy of 'plantation', or settlement of loyal Protestants on land held by them.

This was started during the reign from 1491 to 1547 of Henry VIII, whose Reformation effectively outlawed the established Roman Catholic faith throughout his dominions.

In an insurrection that exploded in 1641, at least 2,000 Protestant settlers were massacred at the hands of Catholic landowners and their native Irish peasantry, while thousands more were stripped of their belongings and driven from their lands to seek refuge where they could.

Terrible as the atrocities were against the Protestant settlers, subsequent accounts became greatly exaggerated, serving to fuel a burning desire on the part of Protestants for revenge against the rebels – whose ranks included a Patrick O'Devlin.

Tragically for Ireland, this revenge became directed not only against the rebels, but native Irish Catholics such as the Devlins in general.

The English Civil War intervened to prevent immediate action against the rebels, but following the execution of Charles I in 1649 and the consolidation of the power of England's fanatically Protestant Oliver Cromwell, the time was ripe was revenge.

The Lord Protector, as he was named, descended on Ireland at the head of a 20,000-strong army that landed at Ringford, near Dublin, in August of 1649, and the consequences of this Cromwellian conquest still resonate throughout the island today.

He had three main aims: to quash all forms of rebellion, to 'remove' all Catholic landowners who had taken part in the rebellion, and to convert the native Irish to the Protestant faith.

An early warning of the terrors that were in store for the native Catholic Irish came when the northeastern town of Drogheda was stormed and taken in September and between 2,000 and 4,000 of its inhabitants killed, including priests who were summarily put to the sword.

The defenders of Drogheda's St. Peter's Church, who had refused to surrender, were burned to death as they huddled for refuge in the steeple and the church was deliberately torched.

A similar fate awaited Wexford, on the southeast coast, when at least 1,500 of its inhabitants were slaughtered, including 200 defenceless women, despite their pathetic pleas for mercy.

Cromwell soon held the land in a grip of iron, allowing him to implement what amounted to a policy of ethnic cleansing.

His troopers were given free rein to hunt down and kill priests, while what remained of Catholic estates such as those of the Devlins were confiscated.

An estimated 11 million acres of land in total were confiscated and the dispossessed native Irish banished to Connacht and Co. Clare.

An edict was issued stating that any native Irish found east of the River Shannon after May 1, 1654 faced either summary execution or transportation to the West Indies.

What proved to be the final death knell of families such

as the Devlins was sounded in 1688 following what was known as the Glorious Revolution.

This involved the flight into exile of the Catholic monarch James II (James VII of Scotland) and the accession to the throne of the Protestant William of Orange and his wife Mary.

Followers of James were known as Jacobites, and the Devlins were prominent among those Jacobites who took up the sword in defence of not only the Stuart monarchy but also their religion.

In what is known as the War of the Two Kings, or the Williamite War, Ireland became the battleground for the attempt by Jacobites to restore James to his throne.

Key events from this period are still marked annually with marches and celebrations in Ireland – most notably the lifting of the siege of Derry, or Londonderry, by Williamite forces in 1689 and the Williamite victory at the battle of the Boyne the following year.

The Jacobite defeat was finally ratified through the signing of the Treaty of Limerick in 1691.

What followed was the virtual destruction of the ancient Gaelic way of life of clans such as the Devlins, when a serious of measures known as the Penal Laws were put into effect.

Under their terms Catholics were barred from the legal profession, the armed forces, and parliament, not allowed to bear arms or own a horse worth more than £5, barred from running their own schools and from sending their children abroad for their education.

All Roman Catholic clergy and bishops were officially 'banished' from the island in 1697, while it has been estimated that by 1703 less than 15% of the land throughout the entire island was owned by Irish Catholics.

An abortive rebellion in support of Irish freedom and independence briefly flared throughout the island in the summer of 1798, only to be followed two years later by the Act of Union between the English and Irish parliaments.

This served to further inflame republican unrest, and it was now that Anne Devlin, born in 1780 in Rathdrum, Co. Wicklow, stepped into the pages of Irish history.

Her family had been supporters of the Rising of 1798 and it was through their connection with the nationalist cause that Anne came to work as a housekeeper in Dublin for the republican leader Robert Emmet.

Emmet's home became the headquarters for a woefully organised conspiracy that resulted in an abortive attempt at rebellion in July of 1803.

Captured and tried for treason, Emmet was executed in September of that year following a celebrated speech from the dock in which he declared: 'When my country takes her place among the nations of the earth, then and not till then, let my epitaph be written. I have done.'

Anne Devlin, meanwhile, had been imprisoned and brutally tortured both physically and mentally by the authorities in a bid to force her to reveal more details of the conspiracy.

But she obdurately refused to betray the republican cause and was eventually released from captivity – but by this time a broken woman.

She died in great poverty in 1851, and is buried in Dublin's Glasnevin Cemetery.

Chapter four:

On the world stage

Generations of Devlins have excelled, and continue to excel, in a wide range of pursuits.

Born in Belfast in 1907, **James Devlin** was the Northern Irish actor whose many British television roles include the 1960s police series *Z-Cars* and, later, the equally popular *Dad's Army* and *The New Avengers*.

The actor died in 1991.

A co-writer and producer of films that include *Universal Soldier*, *Stargate*, *Independence Day*, *Godzilla*, and *The Patriot*, **Dean Devlin** is the former actor turned screenwriter and producer who was born in New York City in 1962.

His acting career included a number of television roles throughout the 1960s, while films in which he appeared include *Bodyguard*, *Real Genius*, and *Martians Go Home*.

Another noted contemporary screenwriter is **Anne Devlin**, born in Belfast in 1951.

A former schoolteacher and daughter of the late Northern Irish politician Paddy Devlin, she is also an accomplished short-story writer and playwright – winning the Hennessy Literature Award in 1982 for her short-story *Passages*.

She won the Samuel Beckett Award two years later,

while her short-story collections were published in 1986 as
The Way-Paver.

Adapted from a novel by Mary Costello, she wrote the
screenplay for *Titanic Town* and also a screenplay
adaptation of Emily Bronte's *Wuthering Heights*.

In the world of music **Adam Devlin**, born in 1969 in
Hounslow, Middlesex is the songwriter and guitarist for the
English band the Bluetones, while **Michael Devlin** is the
internationally acclaimed opera singer who was born in
Chicago in 1942.

A bass-baritone, his professional career began in 1963
with the New Orleans Opera Association, and he has since
appeared throughout the world with companies that include
the New York City Opera.

Devlins have also achieved fame in the highly
competitive world of sport.

Born in Birmingham, England, of Scots descent in
1972, **Paul Devlin** is the former professional European
footballer who won ten caps playing for the Scottish
national team and who, at the time of writing, is assistant
manager of the English Southern League Premier Division
team Rugby Town.

In American football **Michael R. Devlin**, born in 1969
in Blacksburg, Virginia, is the former player who, at the
time of writing, is assistant coach with the New York Jets.

Teams he played for over a seven-year period in the
NFL include the Buffalo Bills and the Arizona Cardinals.

Paralysed in a plane crash while serving with the U.S. Coast Guard, **Christopher Devlin-Young** has subsequently gone on to become one of the world's top disabled skiers.

Born in San Diego in 1961, he was aged 22 when his accident occurred.

Learning to ski at the Disabled Americans' Winter Sports Clinic, he was later named to the U.S. Disable Ski Team, competing in the 1990 Disabled Skiing World Championships in Colorado and winning a silver and two bronze medals.

Skiing in 1997 as a mono-skier, he took both a gold and a silver in two separate disable skiing categories.

A combat pilot with the U.S. Air Force during the Second World War and the recipient of three Purple Hearts and a number of other military honours, **Art Devlin** was the ski jumper who successfully competed during the 1950s.

Born in 1922 in Lake Placid, New York, he competed in both the 1952 and 1956 Winter Olympics. He died in 2004.

On the golf course **Bruce Devlin**, born in 1937 in Armidale, New South Wales is the Australian professional golfer, golf commentator, and course designer who joined the PGA tour in 1962 after an amateur career that included winning the Australian Amateur in 1959.

On the baseball field **Arthur Devlin**, born in Washington D.C. in 1879 and who died in 1948, was the talented Major League baseball player who spent most of his career with the New York Giants, where he started as a first baseman in 1904.

Traded to the Boston Braves in 1911, he played with them until he retired two years later.

In the creative world of art **Harry Devlin**, born in 1918 in Jersey City, New Jersey, is the artist whose cartoon work has appeared in prestigious magazines such as *Collier's*.

Winner of the Cartoonist Society's magazine and book illustration award in 1990, he was also the winner in 1956, 1962, and 1963 of the society's advertising and illustration award and of their illustration award in both 1977 and 1978.

Influenced by the stained glass windows of Chartres Cathedral in France and the work of the Dutch Masters, **Murray Devlin** was the Canadian painter born in 1924 in Vancouver, British Columbia.

A graduate of the Vancouver School of Art, now the Emily Carr School of Art and Design, he was the winner of the Emily Carr Memorial Award in 1955.

Until his death in 2000, he taught drawing and painting at Malpasina Community College at Powell River, in his native British Columbia.

Classed by the State of Massachusetts as a 'stubborn child', **Mark Devlin** was the critically acclaimed writer who was born in Boston in 1949.

His poignant and best-selling memoir *Stubborn Child*, published in 1985, related how as an abused child he nevertheless ended up spending most of his early life in state institutions under a harsh law that defined a 'stubborn child' as someone who 'stubbornly refused to submit to the lawful and reasonable commands of a parent or guardian.'

It was through a letter that he sent to a newspaper in Cambridge, Massachusetts, that his writing talents were first discovered and encouraged, leading ultimately to the publication of his memoirs.

Despite the fame his memoirs brought, the chronically mentally and physically damaged Devlin lived the life of a down-and-out, using public telephones to contact his publishers and conducting interviews from park benches.

He died in 2005.

One of Ireland's greatest modernist poets, **Denis Devlin** was born to Irish parents in the Scottish west coast town of Greenock in 1908, but moved with his family to Dublin when he was aged 10.

He studied for the priesthood but abandoned the vocation in 1927, later entering the Irish Diplomatic Service.

A friend of fellow modernist Irish poet Brian Coffey, he published a joint collection of verse with him in 1930, while his own Collected Poems were published in 1964, five years after his death.

In the realms of the judiciary Patrick Devlin was the influential British lawyer and judge who was born in Chiselhurst, Kent, in 1905 and who died in 1992.

Appointed Lord Justice of the Court of Appeal in 1960 and honoured as a life peer a year later as **Baron Devlin of West Wick**, he was responsible for a number of important legal rulings.

These included the Wolfenden Report of 1957 that established that, in law, popular morality should be allowed to influence law making in order to preserve the fabric of society.

Devlins have also been prominent in the world of Irish politics.

Popularly known as 'Wee Joe', **Joe Devlin** was the prominent journalist and nationalist politician who was born in Belfast in 1871 and who died in 1934 while **Paddy Devlin** was the Northern Irish politician who was born in 1825 and died in 1999.

Devlin, who helped to found Northern Ireland's Social Democratic and Labour Party in 1997, was the father of screenwriter and short-story writer Anne Devlin.

Still active in Irish politics as a founder in 1974 of the Irish Republican Socialist Party, Bernadette McAliskey is the politician who is arguably still better known by her maiden name of **Bernadette Devlin**.

Born in the Devlin homeland of Co. Tyrone in 1947, she had been a student at Belfast's Queen's University when, in 1968, she became involved in the province's turbulent civil rights protests.

Elected to the British Parliament on a 'Unity' platform

in 1969 and serving there until 1974 she was, for a time, the parliament's youngest member.

Loyalist gunmen shot her and her husband Michael McAliskey, whom she had married in 1973, in their home in 1981 – but their lives were saved thanks in part to the skills of a British Army doctor.

Key dates in Ireland's history from the first settlers to the formation of the Irish Republic:

circa 7000 B.C.	Arrival and settlement of Stone Age people.
circa 3000 B.C.	Arrival of settlers of New Stone Age period.
circa 600 B.C.	First arrival of the Celts.
200 A.D.	Establishment of Hill of Tara, Co. Meath, as seat of the High Kings.
circa 432 A.D.	Christian mission of St. Patrick.
800-920 A.D.	Invasion and subsequent settlement of Vikings.
1002 A.D.	Brian Boru recognised as High King.
1014	Brian Boru killed at battle of Clontarf.
1169-1170	Cambro-Norman invasion of the island.
1171	Henry II claims Ireland for the English Crown.
1366	Statutes of Kilkenny ban marriage between native Irish and English.
1529-1536	England's Henry VIII embarks on religious Reformation.
1536	Earl of Kildare rebels against the Crown.
1541	Henry VIII declared King of Ireland.
1558	Accession to English throne of Elizabeth I.
1565	Battle of Affane.
1569-1573	First Desmond Rebellion.
1579-1583	Second Desmond Rebellion.
1594-1603	Nine Years War.
1606	Plantation' of Scottish and English settlers.
1607	Flight of the Earls.
1632-1636	Annals of the Four Masters compiled.
1641	Rebellion over policy of plantation and other grievances.
1649	Beginning of Cromwellian conquest.
1688	Flight into exile in France of Catholic Stuart monarch James II as Protestant Prince William of Orange invited to take throne of England along with his wife, Mary.
1689	William and Mary enthroned as joint monarchs; siege of Derry.
1690	Jacobite forces of James defeated by William at battle of the Boyne (July) and Dublin taken.

1691	Athlone taken by William; Jacobite defeats follow at Aughrim, Galway, and Limerick; conflict ends with Treaty of Limerick (October) and Irish officers allowed to leave for France.
1695	Penal laws introduced to restrict rights of Catholics; banishment of Catholic clergy.
1704	Laws introduced constricting rights of Catholics in landholding and public office.
1728	Franchise removed from Catholics.
1791	Foundation of United Irishmen republican movement.
1796	French invasion force lands in Bantry Bay.
1798	Defeat of Rising in Wexford and death of United Irishmen leaders Wolfe Tone and Lord Edward Fitzgerald.
1800	Act of Union between England and Ireland.
1803	Dublin Rising under Robert Emmet.
1829	Catholics allowed to sit in Parliament.
1845-1849	The Great Hunger: thousands starve to death as potato crop fails and thousands more emigrate.
1856	Phoenix Society founded.
1858	Irish Republican Brotherhood established.
1873	Foundation of Home Rule League.
1893	Foundation of Gaelic League.
1904	Foundation of Irish Reform Association.
1913	Dublin strikes and lockout.
1916	Easter Rising in Dublin and proclamation of an Irish Republic.
1917	Irish Parliament formed after Sinn Fein election victory.
1919-1921	War between Irish Republican Army and British Army.
1922	Irish Free State founded, while six northern counties remain part of United Kingdom as Northern Ireland, or Ulster; civil war up until 1923 between rival republican groups.
1949	Foundation of Irish Republic after all remaining constitutional links with Britain are severed.